ME AND WE

Art by Pallavi Dutta

Me. Me. Me!

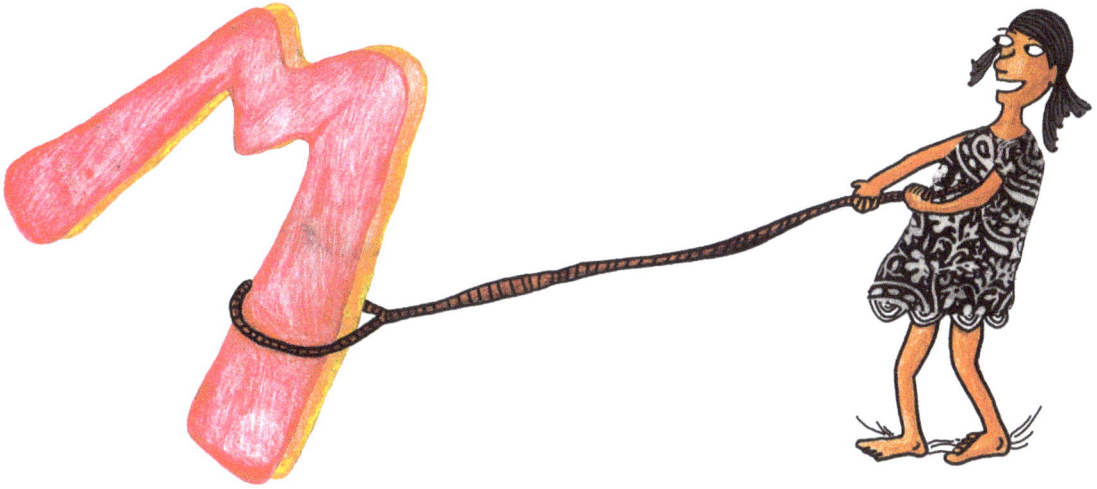

Turn the M around and it is

We. We. We!

I am me.

And you are you.

But together we are

We. We. We!

It is fun to be me.

It is fun to be you.

But it is more fun to be

Meeee-Weeeee!

kindness gets
kindness

A Japanese Folk Tale | Art by Jivya Soma Mashe

One day Azami went to the sea to fetch some water.

As Azami was returning with the pot on her head, she heard a crackling sound. She looked closely and saw it was a fire.

"Fire! Let me run quickly away!" she thought.

Just then she saw a poisonous Habu snake trapped inside the flames. Its eyes looked so sad.

What if it bit her? Azami was scared. But she felt sorry for the Habu.

She quickly put out the fire with the water in her pot. And stood there as the snake disappeared into the forest.

As usual, Azami went to work in the fields the next day.

She was carrying her baby because she had no place to leave her.

So, as usual, Azami left the baby under a tree and went to work.

The baby kept crying. But how could Azami leave her work?

But soon the baby stopped crying.

When the mother went to check, she saw her baby playing with a Habu, happily! It was the same Habu she had saved!

The Habu

smiled.

"You are kind. You saved my life, I came to promise you that no snake will ever harm you or anyone in your family. Ever!"

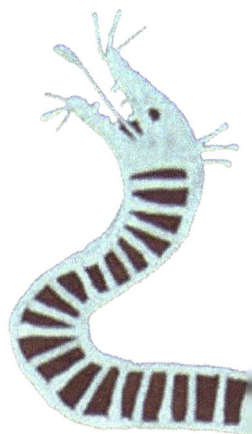

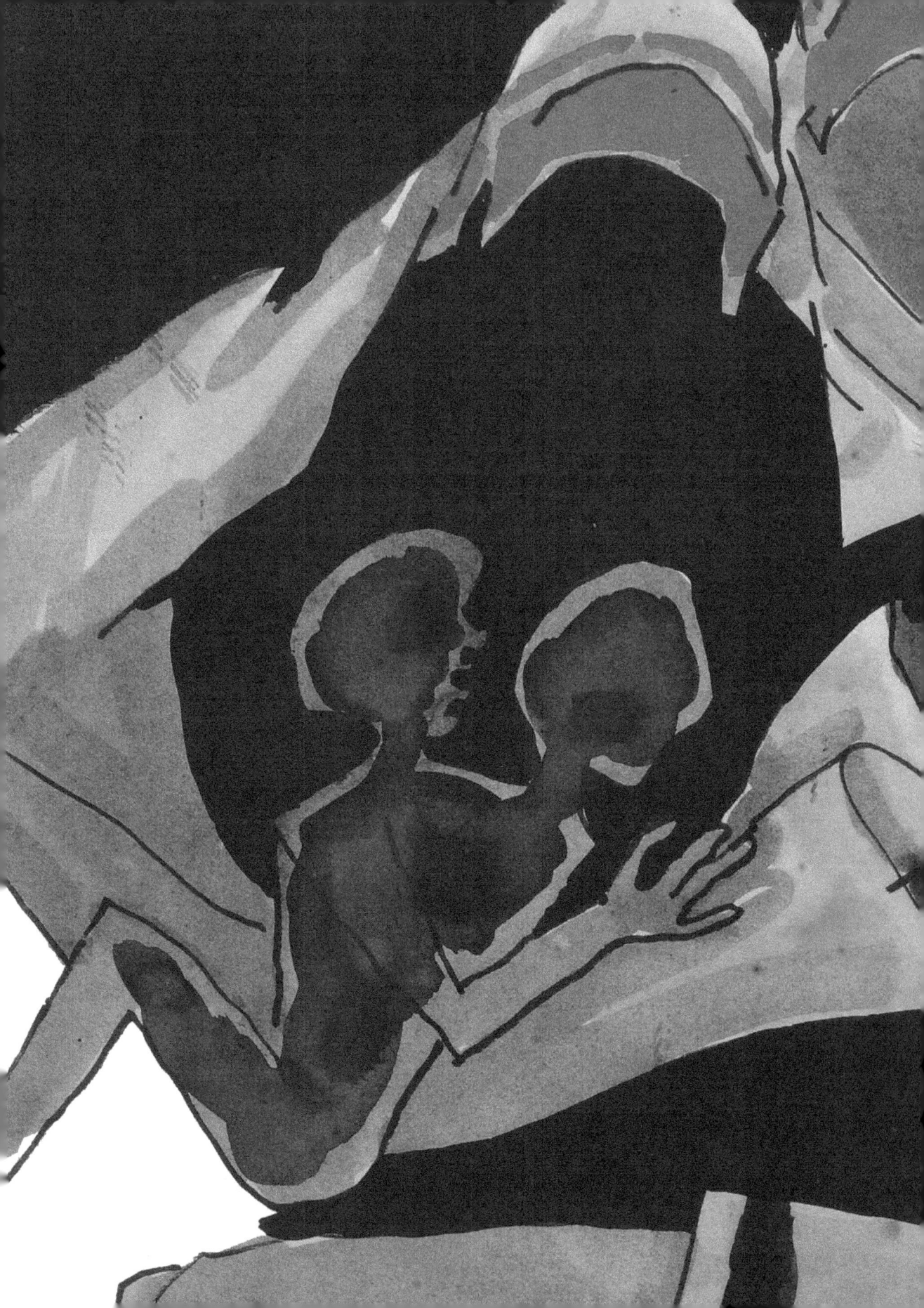

Help One Person

By Mother Teresa
Art by M. F. Husain *(Mother and Child, 1980)*

Peace begins with a smile.

Help one person at a
time and start with the
person nearest you.

THE STORY OF A
HUMMING BIRD

Art by John Gould
(A Monograph of the Trochilidae, or
Family of Hummingbirds, 1880)

A huge fire broke out in a forest once. All the animals in the forest came out and felt very scared, except this little bird.

She said, "I'm going to do something about the fire!"

So she flew to the nearest stream and took a drop of water. She put the drop of water on the fire, and went up and down, up and down, up and down, as fast as she could.

In the meantime all the other animals stood there helpless. And they said, "What do you think you can do? You are too little. This fire is too big. Your wings are too small and your beak is so tiny that you can only bring a small drop of water at a time."

The little hummingbird turned to them without wasting any time and told them, "I am doing the best I can."

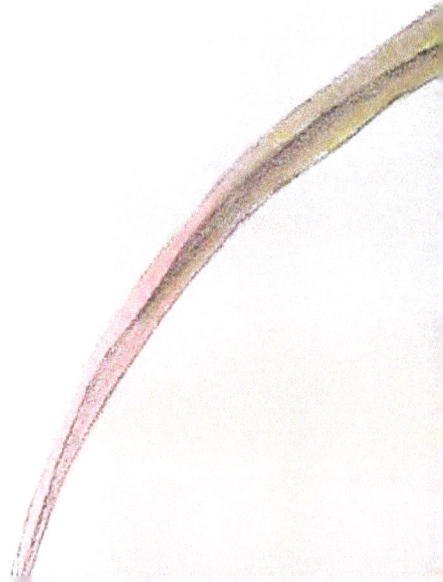

TWO DOCTORS

Photographs by Samruddhi Porey

This is a true story about two doctors — Prakash Amte and his wife, Mandakini.

When Prakash was a little boy, he always went everywhere with his father. His father, Baba Amte, didn't like to see anyone hurt. So he had given up his profession of a lawyer in the city to go and work with leprosy patients. Prakash grew up feeling the same way as his father about people and animals.

Prakash was soon a doctor. Now, he too could help people who were in pain. He and his young wife, Dr Mandakini, went to live in Bhamragad, which is located in a dense forest in Maharashtra. Prakash had been there once with his father. There were many tribal people in Bhamragad, but no doctors at all.

Bhamragad is the place where the people of the Madia-Gond tribe live. They are very frightened of people who they don't know. When they saw Prakash and Mandakini, they ran away from them, deep into the forest.

Prakash and Mandakini built a small hut in the village of Hemalkasa in Bhamragad, close to where the Madia-Gonds lived. And they waited.

They waited three years for the tribal people to show faith in the two strangers from a faraway town.

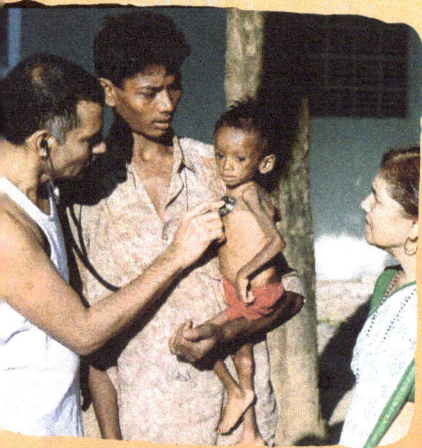

And then one night, Mandakini suddenly heard a noise outside her hut! It was a group of Madia-Gonds, carrying a sick person. "Please help," they said. By now, some of them had realized that Prakash and Mandakini were their friends and would do everything to save their loved one.

As time went by, the tribal people became good friends of the two brave doctors. Some of them helped Prakash and Mandakini build the first hospital at Hemalkasa.

Some years later came a nice school for the Madia-Gond children.

And then, a safe place for orphaned wild animals to live in. It was called Amte's Ark. Soon, Amte's Ark had many animals like leopards, sloth bears, snakes, birds, deer, owls, crocodiles, hyenas and monkeys.

All this happened many years ago. So what is happening today to the Madia-Gond people and Amte's Ark?

Today, Digant and Aniket, sons of Prakash and Mandakini, look after the Madia-Gonds and all the animals and birds in Amte's Ark.

Maybe one day, you will be able to travel to Bhamragad to visit Hemalkasa. Or better still, maybe one day you will be a doctor like Prakash and Mandakini Amte, helping people in remote parts of India to lead healthy and happy lives.

being
kind to our
animal friends!

Art by Suddhasattwa Basu

We should treat our animal friends with respect and must always be kind to them. Here are some things you can do to show respect and kindness towards animals!

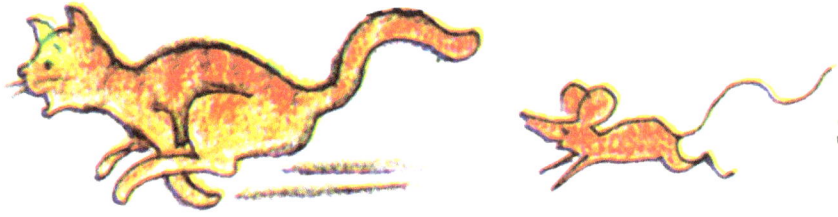

1 Listen to yourself with new ears— don't yell "shut up", "stupid dog", "I hate cats", or other such hurtful things to animals.

2 Never hit animals.

3 Show that you value animals by being patient with them.

4 Give plenty of clean water for animals to drink.

5 Sometimes tiny creatures wander into our homes—help them find their way out.

6 Include animals in your life, and spend time with them!

The Cowherds' Evening Song

A Bodo Folk Song
Art by Haku Shah *(Krishna with Cow, 2005)*

Drive the cows home,
brothers,
do hurry, hurry!
The sun goes down in the west.

Divide them into lots,
brothers,
do hurry, hurry!
Shut the shed-door with care,

The tigress is surely near,
brothers,
do hurry, hurry!
She's sad for her mate is dead.

Do not weep,
oh my tigress.
Don't, please don't weep,
we'll treasure you
when it rains.

Hush! Keep quiet now,
my tigress.
Surely you'll go away,
when the winter is here.

Meet Ajay Gopi, a boy who changed the lives of the farmers for the better!

It's true: age is just a number. Ajay Gopi is all of twenty, but he's helped Indian farmers like none other!

Ajay was born and brought up in a farming community in Mengaluru. His father had to leave farming to sustain his family, and became an electrician. Ajay's parents always thought that he too would become an electrician, but Ajay wanted to do something different.

Ajay was well-aware of the problems faced by the farmers. 90% of the farmers were dependent on rainfall for their crops. They often took loans from banks. And if the rainfall was insufficient, they couldn't repay their loan. Ajay knew that he wanted to do something to change this.

From a biologist friend who'd gone to the US, Ajay learnt about an agricultural practice in which plants and fish grow together in the same farm! Ajay started working on this idea. And soon, he set up a model for his project and started speaking to the farmers.

Ajay's efforts have begun to bear fruit. "Last month, some farmers saw my project and told me, 'We want to set up the same farm, will you help us?'" says Ajay. Of course, he readily agreed.

Ajay's passion is evident as he speaks. "I'm very happy that I am doing good to people. And to myself. I love what I'm doing." he says.

"

I believe one should always do what one loves!

"

THEME TALK

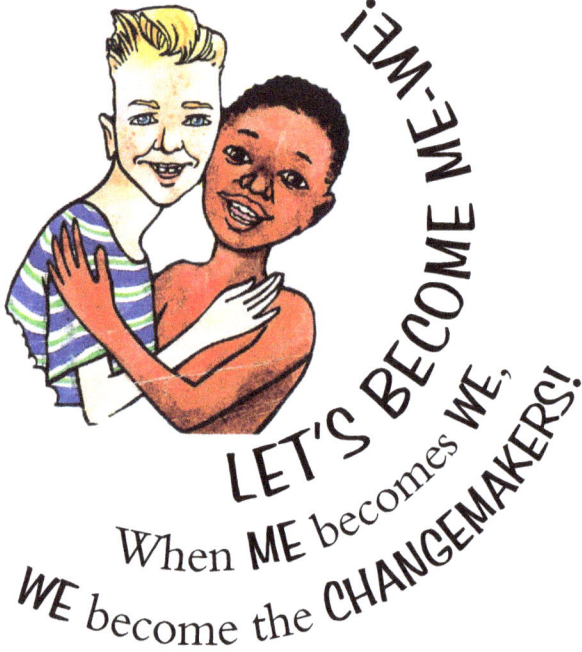

¡LET'S BECOME ME—WE!

LET'S BECOME

When **ME** becomes **WE**,

WE become the **CHANGEMAKERS!**

- We have watchful eyes – when we see someone in trouble, we run to help!

- We have attentive ears – we are always ready to hear our friends out!

- We have a clever head – we know kindness goes a long way!

- We have helping hands – and ready feet!

- And above all – we have a loving heart!

KINDNESS COUNTS

What do you think are the main traits of kind people? List them down.

1.

2.

3.

4.

5.

THE POWER OF KINDNESS

Kindness is a habit. Here are some things you should do every day:

- Take out time to lend a helping hand to someone at school, home, or in the neighbourhood.

- Hold doors open for elders.

- Share your food.

- Help someone read and write.

- Collect old books and form libraries.

- Say 'Thank you' and 'Sorry'.

MY KINDNESS JOURNAL

Make a kindness journal and at the end of each day write down at least one kind act that you did that day in your journal. You can also draw your experiences in your journal!

THE KINDNESS OF TREES

Trees are the kindest things we know! They give us so much, and never ask for anything in return. But are we kind to trees? What can we do to protect our trees?

OUR PRECIOUS PLANET

Earth is the only home we have. Don't you think should all be kind to our planet?

- Be friends with Mother Earth; keep it clean.

- Start a community garden.

- Go green. Plant vegetables and fruits.

- Form Bhumi Clubs and have regular BHUMI SAFAI ABHIYAN!

- Write speeches. Hold meetings. Campaign for your cause!

KINDNESS PITARA

Make a Kindness Pitara (box) in your class.
Write down ideas on how to spread kindness
on a paper. Put it inside the Pitara. At the end
of each week, open the Pitara and read out all
the ideas. Then choose your favourite idea and
follow it for a week!

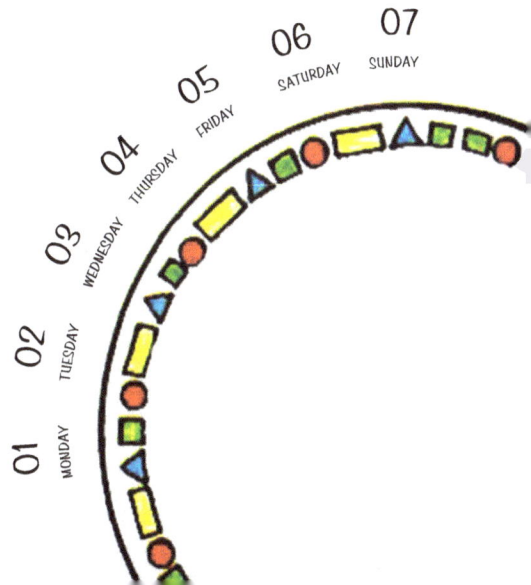

01 MONDAY
02 TUESDAY
03 WEDNESDAY
04 THURSDAY
05 FRIDAY
06 SATURDAY
07 SUNDAY

OUR CONTRIBUTORS

Haku Shah is a renowned Indian painter. He is also an author of international repute on folk and tribal art. | **Jivya Soma Mashe** is a well-known Warli painter from Maharashtra. | **John Gould** was an English ornithologist and bird artist. | **M. F. Husain** was a modern Indian painter of international acclaim and a founding member of The Progressive Artists' Group of Bombay. | **Mother Teresa** was one of the greatest humanitarians the world has ever seen. She was the founder of the Order of the Missionaries of Charity. | **Pallavi Dutta** is an illustrator and a graphic designer. She loves all things visual. | **Samruddhi Porey** is a writer and a film-maker. She is also a practising lawyer in Bombay High Court. | **Suddhasattwa Basu** is a renowned illustrator, painter and maker of animation films for television.

Every effort has been made to trace the copyright holders of the material in this book. We apologize in advance for any unintentional omissions. We would be pleased to insert the appropriate acknowledgement in any subsequent edition of this publication.

KATHA

First published by Katha, 2017
Copyright © Katha, 2017
Text copyright © Katha, 2017
Illustrations copyright © respective artists, 2017
All rights reserved. No part of this book may be reproduced or utilized in any form without the prior written permission of the publisher.
ISBN 978-93-82454-82-3
E-mail: marketing@katha.org, Website: www.katha.org

KATHA is a registered nonprofit organization started in 1988. We work in the literacy to literature continuum. Devoted to enhancing the joys of reading amongst children and adults, we work with more than 1,00,000 children in poverty, to bring them to grade-level reading through quality books and interventions.
A3, Sarvodaya Enclave, Sri Aurobindo Marg, New Delhi 110 017
Phone: 4141 6600 . 4182 9998 . 2652 1752 . Fax: 2651 4373

All stories are by Geeta Dharmarajan, except where specifically stated. © Geeta Dharmarajan, 2017.

Ten per cent of sales proceeds from this book will support the quality education of children studying in Katha Schools.
Katha regularly plants trees to replace the wood used in the making of its books.

VISION PARTNER: ASHOKA INNOVATORS FOR THE PUBLIC

Ashoka envisions a world in which every young person grows up to become a changemaker – a world in which the development of changemakers and the practice of changemaking are the norm – a world in which everyone knows they can change the world for the better, and does so.

ORACLE GIVING

Advancing education, protecting the environment, enriching community life ... and inspiring changemaking in children.

KATHA, a non-profit organization, works in the literacy to literature continuum. We work with poor urban and rural communities, with governments and municipal corporation schools to ensure that every child learns to read for fun and at grade level.

www.ingramcontent.com/pod-product-compliance
Lightning Source LLC
Chambersburg PA
CBHW041634040426
42447CB00020B/3490